TRAINED *to* CONQUER

Teresa Goggins

Trained to Conquer

TATE PUBLISHING
AND ENTERPRISES, LLC

Published by Tate Publishing & Enterprises, LLC
127 E. Trade Center Terrace | Mustang, Oklahoma 73064 USA
1.888.361.9473 | www.tatepublishing.com

Tate Publishing is committed to excellence in the publishing industry. The company reflects the philosophy established by the founders, based on Psalm 68:11,
"The Lord gave the word and great was the company of those who published it."

Cover design by Jim Villaflores
Interior design by Caypeeline Casas

Published in the United States of America

ISBN: 978-1-63122-495-9
1. Self-Help / Self-Management / General
2. Religion / Christian Life / Prayer
14.03.27

PROVERBS 20:18 (NIV)

Make plans by seeking advice; if you wage war, obtain guidance.

This prophetic intercessors manual will train intercessors, prayer warriors, watchmen, and prophetic gifts that have been called to battle in the realm of prayer on behalf of building the kingdom of God, one battle at a time! This manual will carry you through six weeks of spiritual training as we discover how to take our neighborhoods, schools, and cities back for the glory of God! So brace yourselves and get ready to become a qualified soldier in the army of the Lord!

2 TIMOTHY 2:4 (NKJV)

No one engaged in warfare entangles himself with the affairs of this life, that he may please him who enlisted him as a soldier.

Because We Win All of Them

This six week boot camp manual will biblically equip and train its users for the seen and unseen battles in the life of believers. It is also designed to assist those that have been called to pray for leadership and visions within the Body of Christ.

This book is dedicated to my mom, the late Martha L. Weaver, who was the first example in my life of how men should always pray and never faint. Thank you for being such an awesome mom for many years and I pray that you are proud that I obeyed what you asked me to do and that I continue in the faith and complete my assignment while here on Earth. I believe our last conversation when you said, "You have not seen nothing yet." Also to my daughters and husband who always stands by me! Thank you and may God's riches and blessings be upon all of you!

PREFACE

This book is dedicated to all of the prayer warriors and intercessors that are on the field of the kingdom of God every day. Some of you have never been recognized or thanked until now. I want to say *thank you* as one who has prayed many, many times for another man's vision to come to pass.

I know what it takes to stay in the fight when others walk away or just give up on the faith. So I applaud you for keeping the visions of God lifted up around the world, it's because of your watchmen mentally that many battles are won in the church of today! I encourage you to keep going with the same momentum and faith that was once delivered to the saints. This manual was written because of you, WATCHMEN. Remember that you are watchmen for a reason. God put you in a position to build up, tear down, and send warning of destruction to the people of God. So take your assignment seriously during this twenty-first century; you will see a great influx of prophetic intercessors coming on the scene over the next two years.

Position yourself for possession and the kingdom of God will begin to operate in its original intent when Christ gave the power to the church. Lay hands on the sick, cast out demons, rebuke sickness and disease, and they shall recover. His Kingdom shall come on earth has it is in heaven. Stay in the fight because our victory is guaranteed!

The General of the Faith
Co-Pastor Teresa M. Goggins

Spiritual Fitness Pretest

The purpose of this pretest is to determine if soldiers are sufficiently prepared within their spiritual walk with God to engage in battle within the Body of Christ. This pretest will remind you of some of the things that will hinder you on the battlefield. Your opponent knows when you are lacking in any of these areas. Let's begin with the spiritual fitness part of your prayer life as it is today. As you answer the questions below, I encourage you to discuss them with others if needed. This is a great topic for group discussion within assigned prayer groups and ministries.

ARE YOU SPIRITUALLY FIT?

FORGIVENESS

Are you walking in forgiveness with all men?

Answer: Yes or No (If no, explain who and why not)

____

____

____

____

____

COLOSSIANS 3:12-14 (AMP)

> Clothe yourselves therefore, as God's own chosen ones (His own picked representatives), [who are] purified and holy and well- beloved [by God Himself, by putting on behavior marked by] tenderhearted pity and mercy, kind feeling, a lowly opinion of yourselves, gentle ways, [and] patience [which is tireless and long-suffering, and has the power to endure whatever comes, with good temper]. Be gentle and forbearing with one another and, if one has a difference (a grievance or complaint) against another, readily pardoning each other; even as the Lord has [freely] forgiven you, so must you also [forgive]. And above all these [put on] love

> and enfold yourselves with the bond of perfectness [which binds everything together completely in ideal harmony].

Remember...

God will never deliver enemies over into our hands if we walk in unforgiveness among our brethren. Past hurts and pain must be dealt with before entering into a battle zone. Sometimes unforgiveness will cause you to give up prematurely during a fight due to something you should have released years ago. Prayer warriors and intercessors will not be able to pray and trust God with any vision when there is unforgiveness in their hearts. In order to reach the next level, deal with this first and watch God begin to show himself strong in your life. Forgiving others that have wronged you is an experience all believers should strive to achieve.

REPENTANCE

Are you always convicted in your spirit or have a strong desire to repent often?

Answer: Yes or No (If no, explain why not)

____

____

____

____

____

1 KINGS 8:47-49 (AMP)

> Yet if they think and consider in the land where they were carried captive, and repent and make supplication to You there, saying, We have sinned and have done perversely and wickedly; If they repent and turn to You with all their mind and with all their heart in the land of their enemies who took them captive, and pray to You toward their land which You gave to their fathers, the city which You have chosen, and the house which I have built for Your Name; Then hear their prayer and their supplication in heaven, Your dwelling place, and defend their cause and maintain their right.

Remember...

God grants us victories over and over when we continuously repent to him. Even when we are in the most difficult moments of our lives; he always causes us to triumph because we turn to him and repent and pray. As intercessors, you have to wear repentance as a garment for your everyday life. If you've looked at someone the wrong way, always say, "Lord forgive me, I was wrong." It sets you up for a great position in the kingdom of God. God answers your prayers every time when you have repented in the right position for him to hear because the prayers of the righteous availeth much. This prayer is the heart of repentance and having a strong desire to walk up right before him.

FAITH

Do you trust God with your Life?

Answer: Yes or No (If no, explain why not)

____

____

____

____

____

HEBREWS 11:5-7 (AMP)

Because of faith Enoch was caught up and transferred to heaven, so that he did not have a glimpse of death; and he was not found, because God had translated him. For even before he was taken to heaven, he received testimony [still on record] that he had pleased and been satisfactory to God. But without faith it is impossible to please and be satisfactory to Him. For whoever would come near to God must [necessarily] believe that God exists and that he is the rewarder of those who earnestly and diligently seek Him [out]. [Prompted] by faith Noah, being forewarned by God concerning events of which as yet there was no visible sign, took heed and diligently and reverently constructed and prepared an ark for the deliverance of his own family. By this [his faith which relied on God] he passed judgment and sentence on the world's unbelief and became an heir and possessor of righteousness (that relation of being right into which God puts the person who has faith).

Remember...

God honors faith. This statement will assist you through many of life's battles, when you realize that God is on our side and that he desires us to win. We are on the winning team as long as we trust and believe that God is working on our behalf. Never enter into a battle without instructions or seeking the will of God for the enemy that you face. You never want to pray or fight against the will of God, you will lose every time. The key is that faith is a very powerful weapon against the enemy; all we have to do is show up at the fight and trust God to deliver him into our hands.

This concludes the pretest. I pray that everyone passed and are now ready to move forward. If you need to meditate just a little longer on your forgiveness, repentance, and/or faith, this would be a great time to go before the father and get it right. These are just three of the basic areas that will start us on a wonderful journey of enjoying the benefits of a surrendered prayer life!

Let the training begin!

Spiritual Bootcamp

On the opposite page, I have defined some of the positions within our military system as we know today. The US military is trained in intelligence and weaponry and throughout this manual you will be asked to define who you are, who you are fighting for, and why? Once you've realized who enlisted you to become an intercessor, prayer warrior, or a prophetic gift within the body of Christ, then and only then will you stand up and fight the good fight of faith. The armies of the Lord stand at attention!

This is an exciting time as you embark upon strategic instructions to enhance your lives within the body of Christ. We will leave this camp armed and dangerous and equipped to move the vision forward all for the glory of God!

(Compare them to the Kingdom and 5 Fold Ministry)

We can always look at some of these positions within the Body of Christ!

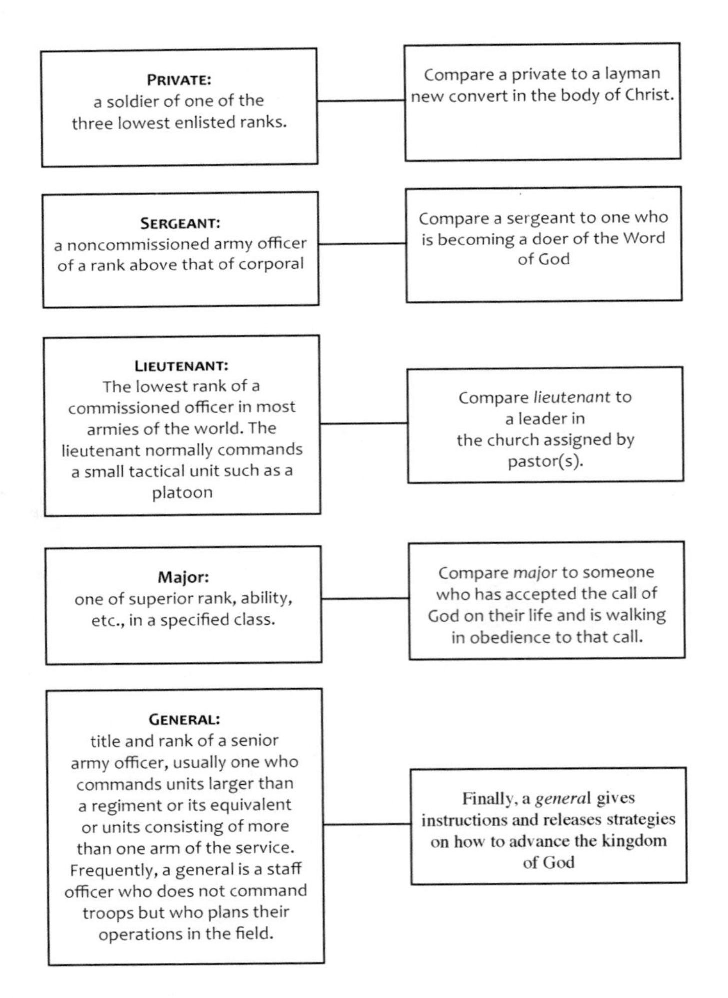

Despite the different rankings, we are all soldiers called to fight in the body of Christ! So let's move FORWARD!

WEEK ONE

WARRING AND WORSHIP:

Learning to fight spiritually and not in flesh

MONDAY

IDENTIFY: WHAT IS THE "WORSHIPPING WARRIOR"?

1 Samuel 17:45-47 (NKJV)

David said to the Philistine, "You come against me with sword and spear and javelin, but I come against you in the name of the Lord Almighty, the God of the armies of Israel, whom you have defied. This day the Lord will deliver you into my hands, and I'll strike you down and cut off your head. This very day I will give the carcasses of the Philistine army to the birds and the wild animals, and the whole world will know that there is a God in Israel. All those gathered here will know that it is not by sword or spear that the Lord saves; for the battle is the Lord's, and he will give all of you into our hands."

We must look at this passage of scripture from 1 Samuel because it's so powerful when it comes to identifying who the worshipping warrior really is. David was a great biblical example for us to follow. He was a worshipper, a man after God's own heart, as well a "giant slayer" on the battle field. As prophetic intercessors we must know who we are assigned to fight for and who called us to the fight. We must always keep our battles spiritual and not fleshly. We must make sure that we always keep pure motives when entering into a battle because we want God to be glorified in all we do and the devil to be put in his rightful place. We know that the battles always belong to God and that we have been enlisted to show up in his name.

WEEK ONE

TAKEAWAYS FOR MONDAY

- Enter every assignment with faith.
- Always come and pray in the name of Jesus.
- Let your opponent know what his destiny looks like and that he will be defeated.
- Never take an assignment or battle personally.
- Always praise God when he delivers on your behalf.

COMMENTS/NOTES

TUESDAY

IMPORTANCE OF RELATIONSHIP WITH THE FATHER

Ephesians 1:2-4 (KJV)

Grace be to you, and peace, from God our Father, and from the Lord Jesus Christ. Blessed be the God and Father of our Lord Jesus Christ, who hath blessed us with all spiritual blessings in heavenly places in Christ. According as he hath chosen us in him before the foundation of the world, that we should be holy and without blame before him in love.

You are chosen! Yes, I said it, even before the foundation of this world. Having a relationship with the father God and Jesus Christ, his son, is what keeps us when we are not on the battlefield or on assignment for the kingdom of God. My relationship with God is what keeps my faith fueled and the fire of the love of God burning in my heart. Intercessors must be totally in love with God because there is no other way. Your love walk must be solid as a rock. Your desire to pray must be stronger than eating, sleeping, or shopping and doing the things in this world that we all like to do so much. God uses us when he needs his will manifested in the Earth realm. He calls on the ones that are committed to prayer and downloads an assignment into their spirits. Glory to God! This is a very important work that we must fulfill while here on Earth, so a relationship with God is top priority!

WEEK ONE

TAKEAWAYS FOR TUESDAY

- Know that you are chosen.
- Seek ye the kingdom of God first and build daily relationships with the father.
- Know that he desires you to come to him.
- Love walk is powerful. One must walk in it.
- All battles are won because of his love for us even on the cross.

COMMENTS/NOTES

WEDNESDAY

TRUTH NOT LIES: THEY THAT WORSHIP MUST WORSHIP IN SPIRIT AND IN TRUTH

John 4:23-24 (NKJV)

But the hour is coming, and now is, when the true worshipers will worship the Father in spirit and truth; for the Father is seeking such to worship Him. 24 God is Spirit, and those who worship Him must worship in spirit and truth.

We can all agree that we must fight spiritually and not naturally in order to win any battles within the body of Christ. I believe this also speaks to our lifestyles and worship life on a daily basis. Intercessors or prayer warriors must live a life of holiness. Your life should always be one of consecration because you commune with God on the behalf of others. We have to stand in the gap no matter what time of day or night or circumstance may be. We must be found ready with nothing blocking us from interceding on behalf of others. We certainly don't practice sin and say that we are called to be the pastor's intercessor or that God is calling you to pray for the vision of a ministry when you haven't figured out how to keep your mouth off others.

Spirit and truth! Live the truth and it will make and keep you free to bombard heaven on the behalf of others. Don't ever lower your standards.

WEEK ONE

TAKEAWAYS FOR WEDNESDAY

- God expects us to be saved and holy.
- Walk after the spirit and ye shall reap after the spirit.
- Be ready to pray and take new assignments ordained by him.
- Live a sin free life (it is possible).
- Worship is a part of who we are.

COMMENTS/NOTES

THURSDAY

AT SOME POINT THE WORSHIPPER MUST GET UP AND FACE THE GIANT!

Samuel 17: 48-51 (NKJV)

So it was, when the Philistine arose and came and drew near to meet David, that David hurried and ran toward the army to meet the Philistine. Then David put his hand in his bag and took out a stone; and he slung it and struck the Philistine in his forehead, so that the stone sank into his forehead, and he fell on his face to the earth. So David prevailed over the Philistine with a sling and a stone, and struck the Philistine and killed him. But there was no sword in the hand of David. Therefore David ran and stood over the Philistine, took his sword and drew it out of its sheath and killed him, and cut off his head with it.

We worship God to get the fuel to defeat our enemies. We always get strategic instructions in the presence of God. That is why David always inquired of the Lord, "Shall I pursue this enemy?" Never take on an assignment that God has not graced you for. All intercessors should be worshipping God every day to hear to this one word: pursue. This is our go ahead to gird up and take over without fail to recover all. There will be giants in our lives but we have to get up off the floor and stop worshipping long enough to take them down. We must learn that when the time comes, there will be a fight going down so draw the battle line in Jesus's high name.

WEEK ONE

TAKEAWAYS FOR THURSDAY

- Take the fight to your enemies.
- Have your weapons ready when you enter the battle.
- Speak your outcome to your enemy and the word of God.
- Know that God is with you by faith you shall have the victory.
- Always give God the glory after every victory!

COMMENTS/NOTES

FRIDAY

THIS WEEK'S WEAPON: THE WEAPON OF PRAISE

Chronicles 20:21-23 (NKJV)

And when he had consulted with the people, he appointed those who should sing to the Lord, and who should praise the beauty of holiness, as they went out before the army and were saying: "Praise the Lord, For His mercy endures forever."

Now when they began to sing and to praise, the Lord set ambushes against the people of Ammon, Moab, and Mount Seir, who had come against Judah; and they were defeated. For the people of Ammon and Moab stood up against the inhabitants of Mount Seir to utterly kill and destroy them. And when they had made an end of the inhabitants of Seir, they helped to destroy one another.

During this six week boot camp, Fridays will be the days we release different weapons for you to utilize while engaging in warfare. This week is the weapon of praise. As intercessors and prayer warriors for the body of Christ, our praise is never predicated on what we are going through or our emotions. We praise God because we clearly understand that it is a commandment and a weapon to destroy the workings of Satan. The Lord will go before you during battles if you go in praising him saying, "I already know that you are the kind of God that will bring me out every time!" I expect to win every time with God. Whenever God moves for us and it is his will, we always win in the end. As we end this first week, we should be blessing his holy name for all he has released in our spirits; he is forever faithful.

TAKEAWAYS FOR FRIDAY

- Praise is a weapon of mass destruction on the enemy.
- God knows the opponent we are about to face.
- Victory every time when we are in the will of God.
- It takes faith to praise God before the victory.
- Praise is a commandment so we must obey.

COMMENTS/NOTES

SATURDAY

MEDITATION ON THE WORD

FOCUS ON THESE SCRIPTURES FOR THE WEEK:

1 Samuel 17:45-47
Ephesians 1:2-4
John 4:23-25
1 Samuel 17 -48
2 Chronicles 20:21-23

The word of God is what makes us powerful weapons. Study each scripture and apply them to your everyday life. Please include your notes on each day and prayerfully you can continue to grow as you awake in prayer, an intercessor inside of you!

COMMENTS/NOTES

SUNDAY

RE-FUEL DAY

"Walk in obedience" to your leadership within the body of Christ and fill the house of God with praise and the glory of God will come over your life. Just watch and see.

WEEK TWO

WHO ARE YOU FIGHTING FOR?

MONDAY

IDENTIFYING YOUR OPPONENT: WHO ARE WE ASSIGNED TO FIGHT?

Ephesians 6:11-13 (KJV)

Put on the whole armour of God, that ye may be able to stand against the wiles of the devil. For we wrestle not against flesh and blood, but against principalities, against powers, against the rulers of the darkness of this world, against spiritual wickedness in high places. Wherefore take unto you the whole armour of God, that ye may be able to withstand in the evil day, and having done all, to stand.

The most important strategy to unfold is identifying who or what you are up against. Never engage in battle ignorant of the devices that Satan will use on you. You are always studied and watched carefully by your adversaries. They know exactly where your weaknesses are and that is what they will work on first. Remember, he goes to and forth seeking whom he may devour. Satan is always watching you; so you should be that watchman on the wall for the kingdom of God, watching as well as praying. Knowing your enemy just as well as he knows you brings you on even ground. Once you have identified who and what you are up against, call it out by name. That is the only way you will be able to take full authority over it. For God has given you power over every power. Glory!

WEEK TWO

TAKEAWAYS FOR MONDAY

- Indentify who or what your opponent is.
- Satan always preys on the weaknesses of a believer.
- Watch as well as pray.
- Call it by name to take authority over it.
- God has given us the power to win each battle.

COMMENTS/NOTES

TUESDAY

FULLY DRESSED WITH THE WHOLE ARMOR OF GOD

Ephesians 6:14-20 (NIV)

Stand firm then, with the belt of truth buckled around your waist, with the breastplate of righteousness in place, and with your feet fitted with the readiness that comes from the gospel of peace. 16 In addition to all this, take up the shield of faith,) with which you can extinguish all the flaming arrows of the evil one. Take the helmet of salvation and the sword of the Spirit, which is the word of God.

And pray in the Spirit on all occasions with all kinds of prayers and requests. With this in mind, be alert and always keep on praying for all the Lord's people. 19 Pray also for me, that whenever I speak, words may be given me so that I will fearlessly make known the mystery of the gospel, 20 for which I am an ambassador in chains. Pray that I may declare it fearlessly, as I should.

There are six pieces of armor. This is also the number of man. God knows how to protect us from Satan's devices and there are many. Paul was speaking so profoundly to the life of an intercessor for we must consistently put on proper armor at all times! Understanding the importance of wearing the whole armor of God everyday of your life will determine your success on the battle field. God has equipped us with all things. It's up to us to utilize what we have been given in the name of Jesus. Make sure that you are fully dressed with the entire armor to get the job done every time. For he who is God always causes us to triumph through Christ Jesus!

WEEK TWO

TAKEAWAYS FOR TUESDAY

- Dress in all six pieces of armor at all times.
- Always pray for each other.
- Pray in the spirit more often.
- We must use what God has supplied each solider to protect them.
- Enter in to win.

COMMENTS/NOTES

WEDNESDAY

PURPOSE OF EACH PIECE OF ARMOR

Helmet of Salvation is the head gear that protects the renewed mind of the believer. You must be born again and saved in order to use this part of the equipment properly. What good is it for a solider to be dressed for war, but have no idea how to use the equipment that they have been given? Cover your minds, Saints!

Breastplate of Righteousness is the protection of the chest area where the heart is housed. If you confess with your mouth and believe in your heart, you shall be saved. This piece of armor protects the heart of the matter. It covers the righteousness that we have found through belief in our hearts that Jesus died for us. We are the righteousness of God through Christ Jesus!

The Belt of Truth is the knowledge that Jesus walks into every battle with us and for us. If God be for us, then who can be against us? Jesus is the truth of God sent to us in human form. Jesus answered, "I am the way, the truth and the life." The belt also holds the armor in place. Most soldiers put their sword into their belts until they're ready to fight.

Sword of the Spirit is the word of God. There is nothing in this universe that can stand against the word of God. The Bible is a sword when used in battle. When we quote scriptures in time of spiritual warfare, it is really Jesus saying those things to the enemy. When you speak the word during battle, you are presenting Jesus as the commander of the fight and it causes the enemy to shudder and run from the confrontation.

Shield of Faith is our faith knowing that God has our lives in full view and that every situation or circumstance that comes against us is under his divine control. You cannot only speak faith or proclaim you trust God, it has to be a way of life. The intercessors must live by faith. For it is: Now faith is the substance of things hoped for, the evidence of things not seen. We live on what we cannot see.

Footwear Gospel of Peace (your shoes) are how you stand on your foundation. Whenever I grab my shoes, it's a sign that I am fully dressed and ready to leave the house. With the gospel of peace we must be prepared to give a word at all times and in all seasons. We must be ready to stand our ground against any outside forces. My feet represent my preparedness. Have you studied to show thyself approved today? What is your readiness in the word of God? When Satan attacks your finances, health or famine sweeps in, will you have a word for him? Get ready solider because he will come and you better be prepared and ready to fight back.

THURSDAY

SEVEN AREAS TO KEEP COVERED AT ALL TIMES UNDER THE BLOOD OF JESUS

I have been an intercessor for many years now. I wanted to share some insight and wisdom with you in order for you to continue being successful while praying the will of God to the Earth realm. Cover the following areas of your life:

1. Mind
2. Heart
3. Belly
4. Eyes
5. Tongue
6. Feet
7. Ears

Keep these areas of your life healthy and you will drive Satan and his kingdom to hell. You will walk in the authority that Christ assigned to the church. His Kingdom will come on earth as it is in heaven.

FRIDAY

THIS WEEK'S WEAPON: THE SWORD, WHICH IS THE WORD OF GOD

Hebrews 4:11-13

For the Word that God speaks is alive and full of power [making it active, operative, energizing, and effective]; it is sharper than any two-edged sword, penetrating to the dividing line of the [a] breath of life (soul) and [the immortal] spirit, and of joints and marrow [of the deepest parts of our nature], exposing and sifting and analyzing and judging the very thoughts and purposes of the heart.

The word is truly the most important weapon. All I can say to this is get full of it. This is the strength and the promise that we have to win every spiritual battle because of our ability and knowledge in God's word. Are you getting an understanding of the scriptures; are you a doer and not just a hearer of the word? We as watchmen must know how to pray as well as warn the body of Christ when the enemy is approaching. The word of God keeps our lives sin free. Intercessors are not sinful natured believers and they can't afford to be. We should always hide the word in our hearts so we do not sin against God.

WEEK TWO

TAKEAWAYS FOR FRIDAY

- The word is living.
- It is a discerner of heart.
- We need more of it in our hearts.
- The enemy understands and obeys the word.
- We should not live sinful lives.

COMMENTS/NOTES

SATURDAY

MEDITATION ON THE WORD

FOCUS ON THESE SCRIPTURES
FOR THE WEEK:

Ephesians 6:11-13
Ephesians 6:14-20
Hebrews 4:11-13

COMMENTS/NOTES

SUNDAY

RE-FUEL DAY

Walk in obedience to your leaders and fill the house with praise and the glory of God will come over your life.

WEEK THREE

THE ORDER OF RECEIVING INSTRUCTIONS

MONDAY

"GOD SEEKER"

1 Samuel 30:7-9 (NKJV)

Then David said to Abiathar the priest, Ahimelech's son, "Please bring the ephod here to me." And Abiathar brought the ephod to David. So David inquired of the Lord, saying, "Shall I pursue this troop? Shall I overtake them?" And He answered him, "Pursue, for you shall surely overtake them and without fail recover all."

Are you after man's agenda or God's? This is very important when you begin to shift into seeking God for divine instructions. Never enter a battle or war without seeking guidance from God. This is critical for intercessors that have been given regions or countries to intercede for. The word clearly tells us to pray for the peace of Israel. Just obey the word when discussing new assignments sent by the Holy Spirit. We must be in tune to hear from God and those that are in leadership to give us instructions on what our next assignments will be. There should be a seeking in your spirit for the things of God every day. Move forward in his presence soldier.

COMMENTS/NOTES

TUESDAY

PRESENCE FOR THE PROMISE

Psalm 16:10-11 (NKJV)

For You will not leave my soul in Sheol, Nor will You allow Your Holy One to see corruption. You will show me the path of life; In Your presence is fullness of joy; At Your right hand are pleasures forevermore.

The more you pray and build a relationship with God, the more you begin to understand what really pleases him. The presence of God brings every promise in your life to pass. It is equally important that we are not lovers of this world. You will either love one or hate the other. Intercessors must be assigned and be experts on getting in the presence of God. This means that we must keep our lives consecrated before the father in order to stand in the gap at any given moment. You never ask which assignments you will receive from God, but we know that you should always be ready, to stand in the gap for others. Holy living is a part of who we are and what we shall become.

COMMENTS/NOTES

WEDNESDAY

SUBMISSION TO THOSE IN AUTHORITY

1 Peter 2:17-19 (NKJV)

Honor all people. Love the brotherhood. Fear God. Honor the king. Servants, be submissive to your masters with all fear, not only to the good and gentle, but also to the harsh. For this is commendable, if because of conscience toward God one endures grief, suffering wrongfully.

Prayer warriors, intercessors, and watchmen on the wall are all under the authority of Christ. So are those that have rule over us; such as pastors, bishops, prayer team leaders, etc. If you have a problem with submitting to those in authority, no need to go any further. The whole fact that God answers the prayers of the righteous is because of our submission to his will being carried out in the Earth. It is not the job of the intercessor to always understand what leaders are doing or the process thereof. Their job is to pray and not judge in Jesus's name. Remember that we are soldiers in the army of the Lord which we are also called servants.

COMMENTS/NOTES

THURSDAY

THE MATURING OF THE INTERCESSOR

Ephesians 4:14-16 (NKJV)

That we should no longer be children, tossed to and fro and carried about with every wind of doctrine, by the trickery of men, in the cunning craftiness of deceitful plotting, but, speaking the truth in love, may grow up in all things into Him who is the head—Christ— from whom the whole body, joined and knit together by what every joint supplies, according to the effective working by which every part does its share, causes growth of the body for the edifying of itself in love.

It is very important that we grow in the things of God. As we spend most of our time in the presence of God, we can't help but to mature. Intercessors will know when their spirits have entered what I call a flesh-lead environment. It is run by man's agenda and God is not the main focus. Most of us dismiss ourselves because we cannot afford to go there. We have to be open to hear from God at all times. We must be liken unto Paul; when I was a child, I spoke as a child, but when I got old I put away childish things. Make sure you walk in the spirit and not in your flesh, because you will reap to the flesh every time.

Move out soldier and declare something!

COMMENTS/NOTES

FRIDAY

WEAPON: RIGHTEOUS LIVING AS A WEAPON

Ephesians 6:13-18 (MSG)

Be prepared. You're up against far more than you can handle on your own. Take all the help you can get, every weapon God has issued, so that when it's all over you'll still be on your feet. Truth, righteousness, peace, faith, and salvation are more than words. Learn how to apply them. You'll need them throughout your life. God's word is an indispensable weapon. In the same way, prayer is essential in this ongoing warfare. Pray hard and long. Pray for your brothers and sisters. Keep your eyes open. Keep each other's spirits up so that no one falls behind or drops out.

There is a mandatory call for intercessors to live right. This is what drives your enemies crazy when your life lines up with the word of God. You stand for holiness and righteousness at all times. This is a great weapon to destroy the workings of your personal enemies. The clarion call for all of God's army to stand up and declare that for God I live and for God I'll die. We should never be dismayed about things that people may inquire such as wealth, houses, cars and other material things. Please don't equate this with the power of God. If I was a chief sinner with a good job and good credit, of course I would be able to get things according to the world's standards. But God's standard is one of righteous walking and talking.

This will be the great deception in these last and evil times. Wealth shall be in the house of the righteous.

Move in solider. Let's go.

COMMENTS/NOTES

SATURDAY

MEDITATION ON THE WORD

FOCUS ON THESE SCRIPTURES FOR THE WEEK:

1 Samuel 30:7-9
Psalm 16:10-11
Ephesians 4:14-16
Ephesians 6:13-18

TAKEAWAYS

- Live a holy life before God.
- Right living can be used as a weapon.
- Acquiring things is not power with God.

SUNDAY

RE-FUEL DAY

Walk in obedience to your leaders and fill the house with praise, and the glory of God will come over your life.

COMMENTS/NOTES

WEEK FOUR

FAITH

Hebrews 11:5-7 (AMP)

Because of faith Enoch was caught up and transferred to heaven, so that he did not have a glimpse of death; and he was not found, because God had translated him. For even be- fore he was taken to heaven, he received testimony [still on record] that he had pleased and been satisfactory to God. 6 But without faith it is impossible to please and be satisfactory to Him. For whoever would come near to God must [necessarily] believe that God exists and that He is the rewarder of those who earnestly and diligently seek Him [out].

MONDAY

FAITH WALKERS & TALKERS

Hebrews 10:37-39

"For yet a little while, And He[a] who is coming will come and will not tarry. Now the[b] just shall live by faith; But if anyone draws back, My soul has no pleasure in him."[c] But we are not of those who draw back to perdition, but of those who believe to the saving of the soul.

Put your lifestyle where your mouth is. Oh Glory! Don't live a double standard life with prayer assignments in your belly. This is a recipe for disaster. In all your getting, get an understanding that we were not only be created in his image, but must live according to his ways and by examples at all times. God would never ask of us what he has not equipped us to do. Those who walk in the authority of Jesus Christ should be operating in the greater works as he promised us we would do. Come on solider, it's all working for our good!

Rise Up!

COMMENTS/NOTES

TUESDAY

A SPIRIT OF ENDURANCE

Timothy 2:2-4 (KJV)

And the things that thou hast heard of me among many witnesses, the same commit thou to faithful men, who shall be able to teach others also. Thou therefore endure hardness, as a good soldier of Jesus Christ. No man that warreth entangleth himself with the affairs of this life; that he may please him who hath chosen him to be a soldier.

Intercessors never give up! We are called to continue to trust, speak, and pronounce the directions and the outcome of God's will. We do that by keeping the word of God's covering on everything and every thought. We know that God has an expected end for all that love him and we stand on just that. Endure until the Holy Spirit reveals the next step in the battle zone. Stay alert and get ready to move in.

COMMENTS/NOTES

WEDNESDAY

ANTICIPATION FOR THE REWARD

Romans 8:18-20 (KJV)

> For I reckon that the sufferings of this present time are not worthy to be compared with the glory which shall be revealed in us. For the earnest expectation of the creature waiteth for the manifestation of the sons of God. For the creature was made subject to vanity, not willingly, but by reason of him who hath subjected the same in hope,

I expect God to move on every situation we pray about. His ear is always inclined to the righteous, so we know he is ready to answer us right away. So anticipate change whenever you have entered to pray at the mercy seat. Something has to change because the will of God will show up. Sometimes it is not what flesh wants, but always expect God to move on the behalf of intercessors that are walking and praying in agreement on the assignment given by God.

COMMENTS/NOTES

THURSDAY

DECREE AND DECLARE, LEARN THE POWER OF SAYING SO...

Exodus 9:16 (NKJV)

But indeed for this purpose I have raised you up, that I may show My power in you, and that My name may be declared in all the earth.

The mouth is where your power source resides. My voice is recognized in heaven and hell. The Power of Life and Death is in the tongue because we have the power and authority to cast out demons and release angelic beings with that same voice. Intercessor, there is a sound that comes up out of your spirit that makes you a global threat to Satan's kingdom. You can build and tear down at the same time. Let's do a practice run...open you mouth right now and declare something and decree it to be so, in Jesus's name. "Reload" and stand at attention.

COMMENTS/NOTES

FRIDAY

THIS WEEK'S WEAPON: THE WEAPON OF FAITH

Lamentations 3:22-24 (AMP)

It is because of the Lord's mercy and loving- kindness that we are not consumed, because His [tender] compassions fail not. They are new every morning; great and abundant is Your stability and faithfulness. The Lord is my portion or share, says my living being (my inner self); therefore will I hope in Him and wait expectantly for Him.

God is faithful to us when we are faithful to him! If you trust your commander in chief, you are ready to carry out orders at all times. God wants us only to believe.

COMMENTS/NOTES

SATURDAY

MEDITATION ON THE WORD

FOCUS ON THESE SCRIPTURES FOR THE WEEK:

Lamentations 3:22-24
Exodus 9 (NKJV)
Romans 8:18-20
2 Timothy 2:2-4 (KJV)
Hebrews 10:37-39

TAKEAWAYS

- Intercessors must have faith in what they are asking God to do.
- Surround yourself with like-minded people.
- Stay consistent; do not waver in your faith.
- Expect God because he will move.

SUNDAY

RE-FUEL DAY

Walk in obedience to your leaders and fill the house with praise and the glory of God will come over your life.

COMMENTS/NOTES

WEEK FIVE

CONSISTENCY

Looking for fame? Wrong Ministry

Mark 1:26-28 (KJV)

And when the unclean spirit had torn him, and cried with a loud voice, he came out of him. And they were all amazed, insomuch that they questioned among themselves, saying, What thing is this? what new doctrine is this? for with authority commandeth he even the unclean spirits, and they do obey him. And immediately his fame spread abroad throughout all the region round about Galilee.

As we obey the voice of God's instructions and enter into the will of God, others will begin to notice that the power of God is certainly manifesting in your life. This is not a moment to seek fame or get out of the will of God. It is time to keep pressing and obeying God. Never get on your own agenda when

God is trying to advance his will through you. The scripture above says it perfectly. People will try and make you famous but your only desire is to keep terrorizing the devil's kingdom. Yes!

MONDAY

"DEMON CHASER"

Mark 1:33-35 (NKJV)

And the whole city was gathered together at the door. Then He healed many who were sick with various diseases, and cast out many demons; and He did not allow the demons to speak, because they knew Him. Now in the morning, having risen a long while before daylight, He went out and departed to a solitary place; and there He prayed.

We cannot get comfortable with the evil spirits in our world today. We must address them just as Jesus did. We need to pray for other nations that are bound up by darkness and continue to spread the light of Christ through our prayers. There is no distance in the word of God. He sent his word and healed all of their diseases. Make sure that we are not coming into agreement with Satan's plans and desires to destroy us. Intercessors are pulling down every stronghold that exalts itself against the (vision of one's ministry) knowledge of God.

COMMENTS/NOTES

TUESDAY

POWER OVER THE POWERLESS

Matthew 28:17-19 (KJV)

> And when they saw him, they worshipped him: but some doubted. And Jesus came and spake unto them, saying, All power is given unto me in heaven and in earth. Go ye therefore, and teach all nations, baptizing them in the name of the Father, and of the Son, and of the Holy Ghost:

Never give Satan more credit than he deserves. The word of God has rendered him powerless. Christ has given us the power he once had; this is the whole problem that Satan has with you. He knows that Christ gave it to you, so now it's his job to keep us doubting that every day of our lives. But intercessors, we know that the word of God is true; so we gladly take our place and begin to line up everything according to the divine will by what we are praying and speaking. Bless the high name of Jesus!

COMMENTS/NOTES

WEDNESDAY

FINDING SATAN'S PLACE FOR HIM

Ephesians 1:20-22 (NKJV)

Which He worked in Christ when He raised Him from the dead and seated Him at His right hand in the heavenly places, 21 far above all principality and power and might and dominion, and every name that is named, not only in this age but also in that which is to come. And He put all things under His feet, and gave Him to be head over all things to the church,

This is Satan's permanent home before his final destination in hell. If he is operating in any other place in our lives, he is illegally violating. He does not have the authority, without permission, and only you can give him that permission. Intercessors continuously remind Satan to release, reveal his plot and cast out, and expose his plan in the lives of God's people! Satan must go so that the Kingdom can grow!

COMMENTS/NOTES

THURSDAY

OBEDIENCE IS A KEY ELEMENT TO UNLOCKING THE KINGDOM OF GOD

Romans 5:18-20 (NKJV)

Therefore, as through one man's offense judgment came to all men, resulting in condemnation, even so through one Man's righteous act the free gift came to all men, resulting in justification of life. For as by one man's disobedience many were made sinners, so also by one Man's obedience many will be made righteous. Moreover the law entered that the offense might abound. But where sin abounded, grace abounded much more,

Obedience is a must in the life of every solider that will enter the Army of the Lord. Christ is our commander and chief and we must obey all of the law, not just what feels good to us. The greatest covering on the battlefield is to walk in obedience. Humility always accompanies obedience. Don't ever lean to your own understanding, but in everything acknowledge him and he will direct you path.

COMMENTS/NOTES

FRIDAY

THIS WEEK'S WEAPON: THE BLOOD OF JESUS AS A WEAPON

Zechariah 9:11-13

"And you, because of my blood covenant with you, I'll release your prisoners from their hopeless cells. Come home, hope-filled prisoners! This very day I'm declaring a double bonus— everything you lost returned twice-over! Judah is now my weapon, the bow I'll pull, setting Ephraim as an arrow to the string. I'll wake up your sons, O Zion, to counter your sons, O Greece. From now on people are my swords."

The blood of Jesus is so powerful in the life of every believer. The blood of the lamb covers every mistake we have made and will make. Intercessors, don't leave home without covering every area of your life. Cover your spouse, children, home, car, etc. Satan will not be pleased that you are now becoming well trained to demolish his work, so he will be looking for an area to attack. However, we render him powerless in Jesus's name.

COMMENTS/NOTES

SATURDAY

MEDITATION ON THE WORD

FOCUS ON THESE SCRIPTURES FOR THE WEEK:

Zechariah 9:11-13
Romans 5:18-20 (NKJV)
Ephesians 1:20-22
Matthew 28:17-19 (KJV)
Mark 1:33-35

TAKEAWAYS

- Important to know who you are.
- Satan must be addressed and properly put in place (under your feet).
- The power of the Blood of Jesus.

SUNDAY

RE-FUEL DAY

Walk in obedience to your leaders and fill the house with praise and the glory of God will come over your life.

COMMENTS/NOTES

WEEK SIX

THE IMPORTANCE OF FIGHTING THE RIGHT BATTLES:

Only fight when it is in the will of God to pursue

MONDAY
TO
WEDNESDAY
DISCERNMENT

1 Chronicles 22:11-16 (NKJV)

"So now, son, God be with you." God-speed as you build the sanctuary for your God, the job God has given you. And may God also give you discernment and understanding when he puts you in charge of Israel so that you will rule in reverent obedience under God's revelation. That's what will make you successful, following the directions and doing the things that God commanded Moses for Israel. Courage! Take charge! Don't be timid and don't hold back. Look at this—I've gone through a lot of trouble to stockpile materials for the sanctuary of God: a hundred thousand talents (3,775 tons) of gold, a million talents (37,750 tons) of silver, tons of bronze and iron—too much to weigh—and all this timber and stone. And you're free to add more. And workers both plentiful and prepared: stonecutters, masons, carpenters, artisans in gold and silver, bronze and iron. You're all set—get to work! And God-speed!

Discernment is very important in the life of an intercessor. Always use wisdom and understanding to study your opponent. Always know what you are up against and bring in the right weapons to destroy your current enemy. Your discernment will assist you with what weapons to use and how to use them. While praying in the Holy Ghost, your discernment always heightens. Remember, spiritual eyes are the greatest sight to have!

This is the final week of boot camp and before we can move out to full assignments in the Kingdom of God, we must deal with this very important principle of discernment. Every solider should have this with them at all times. Spiritual wisdom is the key to conquering most battles.

Pray in the Holy Ghost; it will sharpen your Discernment.

COMMENTS/NOTES

THURSDAY

"DISCOVER HOW TO LOSE BATTLES BUT STILL WIN THE WAR"

Exodus 15:2-4 (NKJV)

The Lord is my strength and song, And He has become my salvation; He is my God, and I will praise Him; My father's God, and I will exalt Him The Lord is a man of war; The Lord is His name. Pharaoh's chariots and his army He has cast into the sea; His chosen captains also are drowned in the Red Sea.

Remember, the Lord is the one that enters each battle on our behalf and defeats all our enemies, "The Lord is a man of war." Most of the time, we just show up and see the salvation. God wants to know if you are willing to trust him and his word for victory each and every time! There are times when it seems like we are losing a battle but know that the war is not over until we win. With Jesus we always triumph in him. We align ourselves with his word and that is what guarantees victory in his name. Oh, Praise his high name!

COMMENTS/NOTES

FRIDAY

THIS WEEK'S WEAPON: THE WEAPON IS LOVE

John 3:16 (NKJV)

For God so loved the world that He gave His only begotten Son, that whoever believes in Him should not perish but have everlasting life.

Love is what gave us the greatest victory of all. Because of God's love for this world, we can now experience his son, Jesus; glory to God in the highest! Love is the most powerful weapon because it covers a multitude of faults and when it is perfect it casteth out fear. The devil is always defeated when we share the love of Christ and love our enemies.

Luke 6:34-36 (NKJV)

And if you lend to those from whom you hope to receive back, what credit is that to you? For even sinners lend to sinners to receive as much back. But love your enemies, do good, and lend, hoping for nothing in return; and your reward will be great, and you will be sons of the Most High. For He is kind to the unthankful and evil. Therefore be merciful, just as your Father also is merciful.

This is what I have to say to you; as hard as this may be:

Love your Enemies!

COMMENTS/NOTES

SATURDAY

MEDITATION ON THE WORD

FOCUS ON THESE SCRIPTURES FOR THE WEEK:

1 Chronicles 22:11-16
John 3:16 (NKJV)
Luke 6:34-36 (NKJV)

WEEK SIX

TAKEAWAYS

- Study discernment it will unlock many doors.
- Love is the greatest weapon.
- Your enemies need to see the Love of God operating through you.

SUNDAY

RE-FUEL DAY

Walk in obedience to your leaders and fill the house with praise and the glory of God will come over your life.

COMMENTS/NOTES

At Ease Soldier

You have just completed six weeks of spiritual boot camp for intercessors! As we begin to prepare for our full-duty assignments to stand and pray for the nations and the kingdom of God, you are armed and dangerous to demolish Satan's kingdom.

Most intercessors are an extreme threat to any of Satan's tactics and plots, as they continue to pray the will of God in the earth realm. Intercession is a very active ministry and you must use wisdom and get lots of rest. My prayer is that you will learn after many victories and defeats the "Art of Retreat." Just learn to pull away, get refueled and get back on the wall. Never be afraid to ask someone to be in agreement with you and trust God until he brings it to pass. I am very excited about what God is doing in your life and every intercessor around the world. We will see life changes around the globe if we all just come in agreement and pray, our land will be healed.

My Final Thoughts

"The Spirit of the Conqueror"

Romans 8:36-39 (NKJV)

Even as it is written, For Thy sake we are put to death all the day long; we are regarded and counted as sheep for the slaughter. Yet amid all these things we are more than conquerors [m] and gain a surpassing victory through Him Who loved us. For I am persuaded beyond doubt (am sure) that neither death nor life, nor angels nor principalities, nor things [n]impending and threatening nor things to come, nor powers, Nor height nor depth, nor anything else in all creation will be able to separate us from the love of God which is in Christ Jesus our Lord.

This is why we Do what we Do!

We love God with all our minds, body and soul. So our greatest desire is to see the Kingdom of God advanced in the earth realm at any cost! This is not a self-fulfilled ministry but one that requires a great level of submission and obedience. The spirit of the Conqueror knows that, "*I enter to win.*" The Intercessor knows that the battles are fixed; I just show up to fight! A true conqueror is so much more than just winning a battle. When you conquer, you rule and reign every day of your life. This word literally means to gain mastery over or win by overcoming obstacles or opposition. The Bible tells us that we are so much more than that, so I do more than just win battles, my personal life is whole, full and complete! *Glory to God!* The spirit of a conqueror does not settle for less than what God has promised in his spoken word. We should not allow the enemy in this world to dictate what or where we stay or pray. We will have dominion and we will occupy until the coming of Christ! If God tells you to rest your tent on any situation and pray, that is what we are going to do, we stay until we see victory in Jesus's name.

It is such an honor to have had this opportunity to share with you. I feel like God is truly moving us into a new dimension in him concerning prophetic intercession. My prayer is that you continue to walk in "The Spirit of the Conqueror"!

POST TEST/ EXIT INTERVIEW

Please answer the below questions, that will signify your completion of *Trained to Conquer* and truly release you into to Great Victories within the Body of Christ!

1. Do you now understand the importance of Spiritual fighting vs. fighting in your flesh? Elaborate:

____

____

____

____

____

2. Can you name some of your weaponry that should always be with you during battles? Name at least three types of weaponry:

3. How important is your Faith when you are a God-ordained Intercessor?

4. What has this manual taught you regarding Intercession that you can share with others?

MY PERSONAL COMMENTS:

Please contact Lady T Goggins Ministries at
ladytgogginsministries@gmail.com or
call us for Training Classes & Workshops
on *Trained to Conquer* 404-704-5197